Liberty Phi

CANCER

INTRODUCTION

Astrology is all about the planets in our skies and what energy and characteristics influence us. From ancient times, people have wanted to understand the rhythms of life and looked to the skies and their celestial bodies for inspiration, and the ancient constellations are there in the 12 zodiac signs we recognise from astrology. The Ancient Greeks devised narratives related to myths and legends about their celestial ancestors, to which they referred to make decisions and choices. Roman mythology did the same and over the years these ancient wisdoms became refined into today's modern astrology.

The configuration of the planets in the sky at the time and place of our birth is unique to each and every one of us, and what this means and how it plays out throughout our lives is both fascinating and informative. Just knowing which planet rules your sun sign is the beginning of an exploratory journey that can provide you with a useful tool for life.

Understanding the meaning, energetic nature and power of each planet, where this sits in your birth chart and what this might mean is all important information and linked to your date, place and time of birth, relevant only to you. Completely individual, the way in which you can work with the power of the planets comes from understanding their qualities and how this might influence the position in which they sit in your chart.

What knowledge of astrology can give you is the tools for working out how a planetary pattern might influence you, because of its relationship to your particular planetary configuration and circumstances. Each sun sign has a set of characteristics linked to its ruling planet – for example, Cancer is ruled by the Moon – and, in turn, to each of the 12 Houses (see page 81) that form the structure of every individual's birth chart (see page 78). Once you know the meanings of these and how these relate to different areas of your life, you can begin to work out what might be relevant to you when, for example, you read in a magazine horoscope that there's a Full Moon in Capricorn or that Jupiter is transiting Mars.

Each of the 12 astrological or zodiac sun signs is ruled by a planet (see page 53) and looking at a planet's characteristics will give you an indication of the influences brought to bear on each sign. It's useful to have a general understanding of these influences, because your birth chart includes many of them, in different house or planetary configurations, which gives you information about how uniquely you you are. Also included in this book are the minor planets (see page 102), also relevant to the information your chart provides.

CANCER

Our sun sign is determined by the date of our birth wherever we are born, and if you are a Cancerian you were born between June 22nd and July 22nd. Bear in mind, however, that if you were born on one or other of those actual dates it's worth checking your *time* of birth, if you know it, against the year you were born and where. That's because no one is born 'on the cusp' (see page 78) and because there will be a moment on those days when Gemini shifts to Cancer, and Cancer shifts to Leo. It's well worth a check, especially if you've never felt quite convinced that the characteristics of your designated sun sign match your own.

The constellation of Cancer is a one of just five stars, with the brightest named Beta Cancri or, in Arabic, Al Tarf which means 'the end'. Hera, the wife of Zeus, placed the crab as a constellation in the skies to thank it for its service helping to save a favourite of hers, Hydra, from destruction by Hercules, which was one of the 12 tasks given to him by Zeus to compensate for his crimes.

Cancer is ruled by the Moon which exerts a magnetic pull on the earth's tides, waxes and wanes and reflects the Sun's light, and its emotional essence is very much embodied by this intuitive sign that feels deeply.

A water sign (like Pisces and Scorpio), Cancer's emotions tend to be very fluid, and sometimes hard to contain. Luckily Cancer is also a cardinal sign (like Aries, Capricorn and Libra), capable of certainty and action, and sometimes in response to what is intuitively understood, which is a great strength. Like the crab, there is an external shell that protects and keeps feelings safe, creating necessary boundaries in spite of their empathy, which means that this sign is no pushover. It is also a sign of great tenacity and endurance, often taking a sideways approach to a problem rather than coming at it head on. Cancer is also gifted with imagination that furthers their creativity and, combined with being an action sign, they are capable of great and successful endeavours.

The sign ♋ of Cancer shows the claws of the crab but can also be seen as two suns connected to two crescent moons, depicting the close relationship between the moon and sun, the light of the sun being gently reflected by the moon's surface.

PHYSICAL POWER
Cancer rules the breasts, indicating their strongly nurturing side, as well as the stomach, which can be as affected by our emotional life as much as by overeating.

SACRED GEMSTONE
The Pearl, which has all the gleaming luminescence of the Moon but also comes from the sea, home of the crustacean crab, and is nurtured in an oyster shell. The Pearl is a gem believed capable of imparting good fortune and harmonious vibes.

OPPOSITE SIGN
Capricorn

There's something a little contradictory about this sun sign. Cancer's feelings run deep but they are so well protected that they might not give much indication of this. That external shell can give the illusion of resilience but for many Cancerians this masks an extremely soft centre, which is easily hurt.

Cancer is also renowned for its tenacity, which those pincer-like crab claws indicate, capable of clinging on for dear life. This can be good when it helps them to stay on task and get things done, pursuing a dream to fulfilment, perhaps, like the action-oriented cardinal sign that they are. But it can also make them possessive and they find it hard to let go – of ideas, material belongings, even friendships – long past their sell-by date. With maturity, however, Cancer can become more discriminating and learn to let go of those things that often no longer serve their best interests. They can also hang on to worries, ruminating over things about which they have little control, way more than is necessary. This trait needs to be managed so it doesn't inhibit their progress, or paralyse them into inaction.

Another aspect of Cancer is a tendency to come at things from an oblique angle, moving in a crab-like fashion towards the object of their focus, making their actions appear a little guarded or secretive. And if offended, Cancer tends to respond in similar fashion, not directly so that the offence is aired and acknowledged, but often passively and with a nip. All of which gives Cancer the reputation for being tricky or moody, but once this aspect of their character is understood, relationships are easier.

Ruled by the Moon, Cancer also rules the 4th House of the home (see page 83) and this can be evident in their commitment to where they live and their family and is often expressed through strong bonds of a maternal kind, whatever their sex or gender. The biggest hug you may ever receive is from your Cancerian friend because they are the most genuinely nurturing of the astrological signs. They are also among the most loyal of friends and always there when needed. This is not a sign that's likely to let others down and their word is their bond, once they've decided you're worthy of commitment.

Cancer can also be uncannily intuitive and especially about other people. This is partly because of their inclination towards close, and sometimes secretive, observation, but this does make them hard to deceive and they can be particularly good at reading another's intentions, even if unlikely to reveal their own until they are very sure of a situation. Cancer does like to play their cards close to their chest, which is what gives them a reputation for secretiveness.

THE MOON IN YOUR CHART

While your zodiac sign is your sun sign, making you a sun sign Cancer, the Moon also plays a role in your birth chart and if you know the time and place of your birth, along with your birth date, you can get your birth chart done (see page 78). From this you can discover in which zodiac sign your Moon is positioned in your chart.

The Moon reflects the characteristics of who you are at the time of your birth, your innate personality, how you express yourself and how you are seen by others. This is in contrast to our sun sign which indicates the more dominant characteristics we reveal as we travel through life. The Moon also represents the feminine in our natal chart (the Sun the masculine) and the sign in which our Moon falls can indicate how we express the feminine side of our personality. Looking at the two signs together in our charts immediately creates a balance.

MOON IN CANCER

The Moon spends roughly 2.5 days in each zodiac sign as it moves through all 12 signs during its monthly cycle. This means that the Moon is regularly in Cancer, and it can be useful to know when this occurs and in particular when we have a New Moon or a Full Moon in Cancer because these are especially good times for you to focus your energy and intentions.

A New Moon is always the start of a new cycle, an opportunity to set new intentions for the coming month, and when this is in your own sign, Cancer, you can benefit from this additional energy and support. The Full Moon is an opportunity to reflect on the culmination of your earlier intentions.

NEW MOON
IN CANCER AFFIRMATION

'Like the energy of the ocean's tides I will trust the
energy of my feelings; they are not final, but help
show me what I need to know.'

FULL MOON
IN CANCER AFFIRMATION

'The Full Moon's light shows me what
I need to let go in order to progress on my journey
and resolve those feelings that might restrict me.'

CANCER
HEALTH

Cancer rules the breasts, the epitome of maternal nurturance, and also the belly organs. In women, the breasts may be vulnerable to benign cysts but also, like one in three women, to possible malignancy, so vigilance in checking for lumps and attending screenings will always be important. The belly too may be subject to over-expansion and related weight gain, as many sun sign Cancers enjoy nurturing themselves with food, leading to an extended waistline.

As an action sign, they may enjoy long-distance running or endurance sports, but Cancer also likes their creature comforts so hours spent pounding along a track don't always appeal. Like the crab, they are at home in water and on dry land, and particularly at the seaside, rivers and lakes, as many are natural swimmers who enjoy water sports. There's an enjoyment of activity that's typical of a cardinal sign, and for some there's an inclination towards competitive team sports, while others may choose to be more cerebral, perhaps by linking body to mind with yoga practice. But few sun sign Cancers are physically inactive, even if they chop and change their exercise options on a whim and do a variety of different activities solo or in a group.

POWER UP
YOUR CANCER
ENERGY

There are often moments or periods when we feel uninspired, demotivated and low in energy. At these times it's worth working with your innate sun sign energy to power up again, and paying attention to what Cancer relishes and needs can help support both physical and mental health.

Reconnect with the water in your sign to power up the body and mind. Swimming in all weathers is often a Cancerian inclination, but even a bath or shower can be turned into something that replenishes a tired soul. There's often a need for self-nurturance to help restore energy, especially after an extended period of caring for others (often the case with Cancer) or working relentlessly hard, and this can start with a long soak using jasmine, vetiver or ylang ylang to scent the warm water. For some, a three-minute cold shower is what they relish to stimulate the body and mind too.

Cancer's tendency to worry and ruminate can lead to depression but fortunately this cardinal sign knows that being active can help prevent this. Physical exercise is a good way to reduce depression and anxiety because it helps raise levels of feel-good hormones, but it also gives the mind something else to focus on for a while which is a useful distraction. Other distractions can also nourish Cancer. Cultural pursuits like music concerts, the cinema, sightseeing or visiting art exhibitions can all refresh a jaded soul, sparking inspiration.

It's not often Cancer will be so distracted that they forget to nourish their physical body through the food they eat, as most know the value of good nutrition and often enjoy the therapeutic process of preparing and cooking food, for themselves or for family and friends. Foods that are high in calcium and magnesium help restore depleted Cancer: wholegrains, avocados, dairy products, leafy green vegetables and bananas are all good. Seafoods often appeal – fish, oysters and even seaweed products – but avoid too much salt. Better to season foods with herbs and spices like parsley, tarragon, cumin, cayenne and black pepper. It's important to keep well hydrated too.

As a water sign, Cancer needs to balance their lives generally and in powering up the physical, this will also help stabilise the emotional. Many Cancers are instinctively drawn towards caring for others so it's very important that they care for themselves too. There's nothing selfish about ensuring the health and wellbeing of ourselves.

Utilise a New Moon in Cancer with a ritual to set your intentions and power up: light a candle, use essential oil of jasmine to lift your mood and energise (this oil blends well with vetiver and stabilising ylang ylang), focus your thoughts on the change you wish to see and allow time to meditate on this. Place your gemstone (see page 13) in the moonlight. Write down your intentions and keep in a safe place. Meditate on the New Moon in Cancer affirmation (see page 21).

At a Full Moon in Cancer you will have the benefit of the Sun's reflected light to help illuminate what is working for you and what you can let go, because the Full Moon brings clarity. Focus on this with another ritual, taking the time to meditate on the Full Moon in Cancer affirmation (see page 21). Light a candle, place your gemstone in the moonlight and make a note of your thoughts and feelings, strengthened by the Moon in your sign.

CANCER'S
SPIRITUAL
HOME

Knowing where to go to replenish your soul and recharge your batteries both physically and spiritually is important and worth serious consideration. For many Cancerians, a home from home is what they look for and they will often carry with them some reminder of home or family, a favourite shawl or photographs of those they love, when they travel. They are not unadventurous but they do like their home comforts.

You could say that Cancer's spiritual home was the Moon, but fortunately there are other options and, wherever they hail from, there are a number of countries where Cancer will feel comfortable, whether they choose to go there to live, work or just take a holiday. These include locations with energy as diverse and attractive to this water sign as Colombia, the Netherlands, Croatia and the Cape Verde islands.

When it comes to holidays, sea or lakesides are often a first choice, but also those waterside cities like Tokyo, Amsterdam, New York and Stockholm. While the watery appeal of these locations is part of the allure, Cancer also likes to pursue a variety of culinary and cultural options too.

C A N

N

W O M A

W

C E R

Many Cancer women epitomise femininity, from their soft curves to their gentle manner, but it would be a mistake to misjudge the backbone of steel that often lies beneath. This is a woman who knows her own mind and, feminine attributes aside, is likely to put in the long hours necessary to achieve her life goals, and she is often very clear about these from a young age. This is not someone who expects to be handed much on a plate either; from career success to emotional solutions, she generally knows the moves she needs to make. This is where the crab's ability to take the sideways moves necessary to get ahead can really pay off.

Sometimes this single-minded aspect of her character can get a little hidden, because she is also likely to be the one in the group making sure everyone else's emotional and physical needs are being met. Luckily that Cancer tenacity helps here, enabling her to focus intently when required and get things done.

This is a woman who's a woman's woman but *also* a man's woman. In fact, when it comes to her friendships Cancer doesn't make much of a distinction between the sexes, which can sometimes be confusing if that friendship is misinterpreted. Loyalty comes as standard in these friendships too, and she's also really good at keeping secrets and her friends know this, and love her for it. The downside to this friendly paragon? There's no doubt that she can be moody but, in her defence, it's the Moon's fault! All those changing energies can play havoc with her own cycle and, if so, learning to pay attention to the Moon's phases will help her factor in the downtime necessary to manage her emotional life more proficiently.

And downtime is necessary because Cancer is also gifted with an imaginative streak, much like her other water signs, and this can mean she needs to pay attention sometimes to working out how best to put her ideas to use. That intuitive streak comes into play too, and her ability to read other people's feelings can sometimes feel overwhelming. Luckily she also has the inner resources necessary to find the balance she needs, often through exercise but sometimes just by immersing herself in other worlds in books, or writing them. Many Cancer women have fascinating secret inner lives that also sustain them.

C A N

M A N

C E R

This man's ability to get things done might not be immediately apparent as he can sometimes come across as a bit of a dreamer, but that's the beauty of being a water sign that's also a cardinal sign. So once Cancer's done thinking through that new shelving unit, the next thing you know, it's up. Whatever their imaginative bent, and it's strong, there's a real practical streak there too.

All of which makes Cancer men some of the best on the planet when it comes to being a friend or work colleague, plus they are thoughtful and loyal, and uniquely able to listen to what someone has to say because they are quite genuinely interested in what others are thinking and feeling. Feelings in particular interest Cancer – theirs, yours and everyone else's. In fact, the feeling side of this man is one of his strongest character traits, and it often shows itself in what he says. 'I feel this is a good idea,' he might say. Or 'I have a feeling you'd like this,' when he offers a suggestion for something you might like to see, eat or do, which is charming of course.

It would be a mistake, however, to imagine that this thoughtful, considerate man is a pushover, because he will only tolerate so much before snapping those pincer claws and letting you know that enough is enough. And if you have upset or offended him, he is likely to retreat into his shell or man cave for a while. He probably will forgive, eventually, but he does have a tendency to hold on to past hurts and slights and isn't always able to completely forget.

Cancer also takes his role as protector seriously. You may not want to be protected, but it's his instinct to make sure those he cares about are cherished and provided for. If he becomes a parent, then his protective streak is likely to be very strong, and he may have to learn to let his progeny go or make their own mistakes, which can be hard for Cancer. This is partly because this sign is not only very invested in the home and family, but also in their ancestral forebears and the legacy they will leave.

CANCER IN
LOVE

R uled by the Moon, Cancer can be quite the romantic
when it comes to looking for love, with a lot of thoughtful
gestures, from flowers and gifts to cooking a favourite meal,
and they seldom pass up a birthday or Valentine's Day to make the
object of their affections feel special. Given this, it can be a surprise
to find that Cancer can also be surprisingly cautious, taking a while
to be sure about how they feel before making a move. So Cancer
often establishes a friendship first, before moving – inevitably with
a sideways movement – on to a romantic relationship, although the
longer this stage goes on for, the less likely it is to change. And they
seldom date purely for the fun of it, given their longer-term goal is
likely to be a home and family, to which they expect a partner to be
as equally committed.

CANCER AS
A LOVER

Empathetic and intuitive, Cancer likes to tune in to their lover's needs and this is one way in which they can also meet their own. Whether the mood is playful or darkly erotic, they will match it. Above all, making love is all about the feelings, both bodily and emotionally, and responding to this. As lovers, foreplay for Cancer tends to start at the moment of meeting, walking through the park, over dinner or driving home, with lots of focus and attention before actually making love.

But Cancer can also be very vulnerable to criticism, despite their protective shell of outward confidence and finesse. And as the Moon needs the Sun's light to shine, so too do Cancers need to know that they are valued and appreciated. They also need to trust this because love and security are inextricably linked, and Cancer needs to feel secure in order to love fully. And the more secure they are, the more confident they feel. Casual sex doesn't tend to appeal to a sign that experiences making love as an emotional rather than just a physical event, and although they rationally accept that not everyone can be *the* one great love, basically that's what they need to feel at the time.

That's not to say it's always intense – when they do feel secure enough to express their feelings fully, there's a delightfully playful and light-hearted side to Cancer. While the crab always needs to keep close to the sea, as Cancer does to their feelings, they are comfortable on land and this helps ground them into the reality of relationships. Once smitten, however, they find it difficult to ever let a lover go, even when a relationship is over, but are capable of moving back into the friendship zone, just as long as the damage hasn't been too deep.

WHICH SIGN
SUITS CANCER?

In relationships with Cancer, the sun sign of the other person and the ruling planet of that sign can bring out the best, or sometimes the worst, in a lover. Knowing what might spark, smoulder or suffocate love is worth closer investigation, but always remember that sun sign astrology is only a starting point for any relationship.

CANCER
AND ARIES

Both are cardinal, action-oriented signs which work well together, but Aries' Mars energy can sometimes overwhelm Cancer's gentler Moon, although there's a nice loyalty between the two that can make their love watertight.

CANCER
AND TAURUS

Cancer's Moon can be greatly enamoured of Taurus' beautiful Venus vibes, finding their earthy energy helps to make them feel secure enough to really shine, while the bull often thrives in a more feeling atmosphere.

CANCER AND
GEMINI

Airy Mercury tends to run happy rings around the gentler Moon, so although there can be an initial enthrallment between the two signs that creates a lot of sexy communication, Gemini tends to make Cancer feel too insecure to commit.

CANCER
AND CANCER

There's an initial welcome recognition when two Moons meet, making them both feel secure, but unless they can reconcile their similarities, there may not be enough room in the relationship for them both to shine.

CANCER
AND LEO

The Sun rules Leo and the Moon can happily reflect the lovely, playful energy this sign radiates, but for this relationship to survive, it depends on whether the lion's exuberant ego doesn't undermine the crab's need to feel secure.

CANCER
AND VIRGO

The earthiness of Virgo provides a secure hold for Cancer, which often forms a good basis for this relationship, while their Moon is happy to listen to and reflect on the mercurial ideas of this more practical sign.

CANCER
AND LIBRA

Libra's constant striving for balance can sometimes seem too vacillating and ambivalent for Cancer, whose Moon needs planet Venus to be more consistent and accommodating to the home and family life in which they thrive.

CANCER AND
SCORPIO

Two deeply imaginative and secretive souls can find solace in this union, and both recognise the need to make the other feel secure in order to thrive, but there is a dark edge to Pluto that the Moon can sometimes struggle with.

CANCER AND
SAGITTARIUS

Jupiter's positive benevolent energy makes Sagittarius an attractive proposition to those ruled by the Moon, but unless Cancer can learn to tolerate their thirst for emotional and physical travel and adventure, they will struggle to commit.

CANCER AND CAPRICORN

Often a very happy union because Capricorn's Saturn is the sort of steady planetary influence that the Cancer's Moon welcomes, although the crab needs to learn that the goat's self-reliance isn't necessarily a lack of commitment to the relationship.

CANCER AND AQUARIUS

Aquarius may be a little too detached and involved in the world's bigger problems, thanks to their ruling planet Uranus, for Cancer to feel important enough to the relationship, so the water carrier needs to make their commitment crystal clear.

CANCER AND PISCES

Often very compatible with both the Moon and Neptune's links to the sea, and imaginative enough to encourage each other's dreams, although it's important that their wateriness is tempered with action for them to thrive together.

CANCER AT
WORK

To say that Cancer enjoys work is probably an understatement because they are a cardinal sign and are all about putting their ideas into action. Their tenacity also means they will often graft until the job is done, and as part of a team can be relied on to deliver. Cancer is happiest in work that reflects their talents and this can include a talent for caring for people, often leading them into caring professions like nursing, and midwifery in particular, social work, student counselling (Cancer is often very good at relating to young people) or teaching.

In fact, their maternal instinct can come across quite strongly in whatever profession they work in, often making them an excellent boss. What Cancer may well have to guard against, perhaps, is allowing their empathetic nature to override their decision-making, particularly when they are in leadership roles. Sometimes a boss has to make difficult decisions that might alienate others, but this can be part of the job and where learning to keep a professional distance is sometimes essential. At times like these, a crab's shell can be invaluable.

Cancer may not find their chosen profession immediately, particularly when it comes to compiling a skill set that helps them into an area in which they have a particular interest, because they are often drawn towards more creative industries that require acquiring specific knowledge. However, they are smart enough to know that progression isn't always linear and a crab's instinct for sideways movement can help in acquiring the experience they need to build their professional profile.

Work will always feature strongly in Cancer's life and it is one of the signs that has the discipline to work well for themselves or from home, often having quite an entrepreneurial streak. Cancer is happy to work hard but expects to be remunerated accordingly and promoted in return for good service, otherwise they will move on. Even when juggling family life they are likely to be successful at working towards a secure income and future and are likely to be financially successful because they are often canny with money, holding on to it and investing wisely, often in solid investments like property.

CANCER AT
HOME

Cancer rules the 4th astrological House of the home: it's where their heart is and they will always seek to create a secure home for themselves and their family. Cancer can also be quite invested in the representation of home, the actual bricks and mortar, and may hang on to a family home long after the family has gone or seek to recreate it in a new location. For them, home is not just a word but an embodiment of all it represents in terms of security. A home may be the first major purchase Cancer makes in adult life. Even if it's a studio apartment straight out of college, they would much prefer to buy than rent and may even sacrifice holidays or new clothes to achieve this.

True to their astrological sign, there may be an indication that Cancer is a water sign in their ocean-blue front door or their interior decor, with aquamarine linen curtains, nautical themes, seascape canvases on the walls or an aquarium, and the bathroom too may be decorated with seashell motifs. It's an unusual Cancerian that doesn't give some indication they are a water sign, and if it's not present in the house, there may be a water feature in the garden.

Their home is also where they like to welcome others and socialise, and it's likely that the kitchen is as welcoming as any other room in the house, as this is where they can cook for family and guests alike. They are unlikely to be pretentious cooks either. What matters is not what the food looks like, but how it makes you feel: nourished and contained and securely fed. It's one of the ways Cancer shows its commitment to those they love: in practical, cherishing ways.

FREE THE
SPIRIT

Understanding your own sun sign astrology is only part of the picture. It provides you with a template to examine and reflect on your own life's journey but also the context for this through your relationships with others, intimate or otherwise, and within the culture and environment in which you live.

Throughout time, the Sun and planets of our universe have kept to their paths and astrologers have used this ancient wisdom to understand the pattern of the universe. In this way, astrology is a tool to utilise these wisdoms, a way of helping make sense of the energies we experience as the planets shift in our skies.

'A physician without a knowledge of astrology has no right to call himself a physician,' said Hippocrates, the Greek physician born in 460 BC, who understood better than anyone how these psychic energies worked. As did Carl Jung, the 20th-century philosopher and psychoanalyst, because he said, 'Astrology represents the summation of all the psychological knowledge of antiquity.'

SUN

Although the Sun is officially a star, for the purpose of astrology it's considered a planet. It is also the centre of our universe and gives us both light and energy; our lives are dependent on it and it embodies our creative life force. As a life giver, the Sun is considered a masculine entity, the patriarch and ruler of the skies. Our sun sign is where we start our astrological journey whichever sign it falls in, and as long as we know which day of which month we were born, we have this primary knowledge.

MOON

RULES THE ASTROLOGICAL SIGN OF CANCER

We now know that the Moon is actually a natural satellite of the Earth (the third planet from the sun) rather than a planet but is considered such for the purposes of astrology. It's dependent on the Sun for its reflected light, and it is only through their celestial relationship that we can see it. In this way, the Moon in each of our birth charts depicts the feminine energy to balance the masculine sun's life force, the ying to its yang. It is not an impotent or subservient presence, particularly when you consider how it gives the world's oceans their tides, the relentless energy of the ebb and flow powering up the seas. The Moon's energy also helps illuminate our unconscious desires, helping to bring these to the service of our self-knowledge.

MERCURY

RULES THE ASTROLOGICAL SIGNS OF GEMINI AND VIRGO

Mercury, messenger of the gods, has always been associated with speed and agility, whether in body or mind. Because of this, Mercury is considered to be the planet of quick wit and anything requiring verbal dexterity and the application of intelligence. Those with Mercury prominent in their chart love exchanging and debating ideas and telling stories (often with a tendency to embellish the truth of a situation), making them prominent in professions where these qualities are valuable.

Astronomically, Mercury is the closest planet to the sun and moves around a lot in our skies. What's also relevant is that several times a year Mercury appears to be retrograde (see page 99) which has the effect of slowing down or disrupting its influence.

VENUS

RULES THE ASTROLOGICAL SIGNS OF TAURUS AND LIBRA

The goddess of beauty, love and pleasure. Venus is
the second planet from the sun and benefits from
this proximity, having received its positive vibes.
Depending on which astrological sign Venus falls in
your chart will influence how you relate to art and
culture and the opposite sex. The characteristics of
this sign will tell you all you need to know about
what you aspire to, where you seek and how you
experience pleasure, along with the types of lover you
attract. Again, partly depending on where it's placed,
Venus can sometimes increase self-indulgence which
can be a less positive aspect of a hedonistic life.

MARS

RULES THE ASTROLOGICAL SIGN OF ARIES

This big, powerful planet is fourth from the sun
and exerts an energetic force, powering up the
characteristics of the astrological sign in which it
falls in your chart. This will tell you how you assert
yourself, whether your anger flares or smoulders,
what might stir your passion and how you express
your sexual desires. Mars will show you what works
best for you to turn ideas into action, the sort of
energy you might need to see something through
and how your independent spirit can be most
effectively engaged.

JUPITER

RULES THE ASTROLOGICAL SIGN OF SAGITTARIUS

Big, bountiful Jupiter is the largest planet in our solar system and fifth from the sun. It heralds optimism, generosity and general benevolence. Whichever sign Jupiter falls in in your chart is where you will find the characteristics for your particular experience of luck, happiness and good fortune. Jupiter will show you which areas to focus on to gain the most and best from your life. Wherever Jupiter appears in your chart it will bring a positive influence and when it's prominent in our skies we all benefit.

SATURN

RULES THE ASTROLOGICAL SIGN OF CAPRICORN

Saturn is considered akin to Old Father Time, with
all the patience, realism and wisdom that archetype
evokes. Sometimes called the taskmaster of the skies,
its influence is all about how we handle responsibility
and it requires that we graft and apply ourselves in
order to learn life's lessons. The sixth planet from the
sun, Saturn's 'return' (see page 100) to its place in an
individual's birth chart occurs approximately every
28 years. How self-disciplined you are about
overcoming opposition or adversity will be
influenced by the characteristics of the sign in which
this powerful planet falls in your chart.

URANUS

RULES THE ASTROLOGICAL SIGN OF AQUARIUS

The seventh planet from the sun, Uranus is the
planet of unpredictability, change and surprise, and
whether you love or loathe the impact of Uranus
will depend in part on which astrological sign it
influences in your chart. How you respond to its
influence is entirely up to the characteristics of the
sign it occupies in your chart. Whether you see the
change it heralds as a gift or a curse is up to you, but
because it takes seven years to travel through a sign,
its presence in a sign can influence a generation.

NEPTUNE

Neptune ruled the sea, and this planet is all about deep waters of mystery, imagination and secrets. It's also representative of our spiritual side so the characteristics of whichever astrological sign it occupies in your chart will influence how this plays out in your life. Neptune is the eighth planet from the sun and its influence can be subtle and mysterious. The astrological sign in which it falls in your chart will indicate how you realise your vision, dream and goals. The only precaution is if it falls in an equally watery sign, creating a potential difficulty in distinguishing between fantasy and reality.

PLUTO

Pluto is the furthest planet from the sun and exerts a regenerative energy that transforms but often requires destruction to erase what's come before in order to begin again. Its energy often lies dormant and then erupts, so the astrological sign in which it falls will have a bearing on how this might play out in your chart. Transformation can be very positive but also very painful. When Pluto's influence is strong, change occurs and how you react or respond to this will be very individual. Don't fear it, but reflect on how to use its energy to your benefit.

YOUR SUN SIGN

Your sun or zodiac sign is the one in which you were born, determined by the date of your birth. Your sun sign is ruled by a specific planet. For example, Cancer is ruled by the Moon but Gemini by Mercury, so we already have the first piece of information and the first piece of our individual jigsaw puzzle.

The next piece of the jigsaw is understanding that the energy of a particular planet in your birth chart (see page 78) plays out via the characteristics of the astrological sign in which it's positioned, and this is hugely valuable in understanding some of the patterns of your life. You may have your Sun in Cancer, and a good insight into the characteristics of this sign, but what if you have Neptune in Leo? Or Venus in Aries? Uranus in Virgo? Understanding the impact of these influences can help you reflect on the way you react or respond and the choices you can make, helping to ensure more positive outcomes.

If, for example, with Uranus in Taurus you are resistant to change, remind yourself that change is inevitable and can be positive, allowing you to work with it rather than against its influence. If you have Neptune in Virgo, it will bring a more spiritual element to this practical earth sign, while Mercury in Aquarius will enhance the predictive element of your analysis and judgement. The scope and range and useful aspect of having this knowledge is just the beginning of how you can utilise astrology to live your best life.

PLANETS IN TRANSIT

In addition, the planets do not stay still. They are said to transit (move) through the course of an astrological year. Those closest to us, like Mercury, transit quite regularly (every 88 days), while those further away, like Pluto, take much longer, in this case 248 years to come full circle. So the effects of each planet can vary depending on their position and this is why we hear astrologers talk about someone's Saturn return (see page 100), Mercury retrograde (see page 99) or about Capricorn (or other sun sign) 'weather'. This is indicative of an influence that can be anticipated and worked with and is both universal and personal. The shifting positions of the planets bring an influence to bear on each of us, linked to the position of our own planetary influences and how these have a bearing on each other. If you understand the nature of these planetary influences you can begin to work with, rather than against, them and this information can be very much to your benefit.

First, though, you need to take a look at the component parts of astrology, the pieces of your personal jigsaw, then you'll have the information you need to make sense of how your sun sign might be affected during the changing patterns of the planets.

YOUR BIRTH CHART

With the date, time and place of birth, you can easily find out where your (or anyone else's) planets are positioned from an online astrological chart programme (see page 110). This will give you an exact sun sign position, which you probably already know, but it can also be useful if you think you were born 'on the cusp' because it will give you an *exact* indication of what sign you were born in. In addition, this natal chart will tell you your Ascendant sign, which sign your Moon is in, along with the other planets specific to your personal and completely individual chart and the Houses (see page 81) in which the astrological signs are positioned.

A birth chart is divided into 12 sections, representing each of the 12 Houses (see pages 82–85) with your Ascendant or Rising sign always positioned in the 1st House, and the other 11 Houses running counter-clockwise from one to 12.

ASCENDANT OR RISING SIGN

Your Ascendant is a first, important part of the complexity of an individual birth chart. While your sun sign gives you an indication of the personality you will inhabit through the course of your life, it is your Ascendant or Rising sign – which is the sign rising at the break of dawn on the Eastern horizon at the time and on the date of your birth – that often gives a truer indication of how you will project your personality and consequently how the world sees you. So even though you were born a sun sign Cancer, whatever sign your Ascendant is in, for example Aries, will be read through the characteristics of this astrological sign.

Your Ascendant is always in your 1st House, which is the House of the Self (see page 82) and the other houses always follow the same consecutive astrological order. So if, for example, your Ascendant is Leo, then your second house is in Virgo, your third house in Libra, and so on. Each house has its own characteristics but how these will play out in your individual chart will be influenced by the sign positioned in it.

Opposite your Ascendant is your Descendant sign, positioned in the 7th House (see page 84) and this shows what you look for in a partnership, your complementary 'other half' as it were. There's always something intriguing about what the Descendant can help us to understand, and it's worth knowing yours and being on the lookout for it when considering a long-term marital or business partnership.

THE 12 HOUSES

While each of the 12 Houses represent different aspects of our lives, they are also ruled by one of the 12 astrological signs, giving each house its specific characteristics. When we discover, for example, that we have Capricorn in the 12th House, this might suggest a pragmatic or practical approach to spirituality. Or, if you had Gemini in your 6th House, this might suggest a rather airy approach to organisation.

1st HOUSE

RULED BY ARIES

The first impression you give walking into a room, how you like to be seen, your sense of self and the energy with which you approach life.

2nd HOUSE

RULED BY TAURUS

What you value, including what you own that provides your material security; your self-value and work ethic, how you earn your income.

3rd HOUSE

RULED BY GEMINI

How you communicate through words, deeds and gestures; also how you learn and function in a group, including within your own family.

4 TH HOUSE

RULED BY CANCER

This is about your home, your security
and how you take care of yourself and
your family; and also about those family
traditions you hold dear.

5 TH HOUSE

RULED BY LEO

Creativity in all its forms, including fun
and eroticism, intimate relationships and
procreation, self-expression
and positive fulfilment.

6 TH HOUSE

RULED BY VIRGO

How you organise your daily routine, your
health, your business affairs, and how you
are of service to others, from those
in your family to the workplace.

7 TH HOUSE

RULED BY LIBRA

This is about partnerships and shared goals, whether marital or in business, and what we look for in these to complement ourselves.

8 TH HOUSE

RULED BY SCORPIO

Regeneration, through death and rebirth, and also our legacy and how this might be realised through sex, procreation and progeny.

9 TH HOUSE

RULED BY SAGITTARIUS

Our world view, cultures outside our own and the bigger picture beyond our immediate horizon, to which we travel either in body or mind.

10TH HOUSE

RULED BY CAPRICORN

Our aims and ambitions in life, what we aspire to and what we're prepared to do to achieve it; this is how we approach our working lives.

11TH HOUSE

RULED BY AQUARIUS

The house of humanity and our friendships, our relationships with the wider world, our tribe or group to which we feel an affiliation.

12TH HOUSE

RULED BY PISCES

Our spiritual side resides here. Whether this is religious or not, it embodies our inner life, beliefs and the deeper connections we forge.

THE FOUR
ELEMENTS

The 12 astrological signs are divided into four groups, representing the four elements: fire, water, earth and air. This gives each of the three signs in each group additional characteristics.

FIRE

ARIES ❧ LEO ❧ SAGITTARIUS

Embodying warmth, spontaneity and enthusiasm.

WATER

CANCER ❧ SCORPIO ❧ PISCES

Embody a more feeling, spiritual and intuitive side.

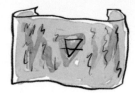

EARTH

TAURUS ❧ VIRGO ❧ CAPRICORN

Grounded and sure-footed and sometimes rather stubborn.

CANCER

AIR

GEMINI ❧ LIBRA ❧ AQUARIUS

Flourishing in the world of vision, ideas and perception.

FIXED,
CARDINAL OR
MUTABLE?

The 12 signs are further divided into three groups of four, giving additional characteristics of being fixed, cardinal or mutable. These represent the way in which they respond to situations.

FIXED

TAURUS, LEO, SCORPIO AND AQUARIUS ARE FIXED SIGNS

Their energy tends to be steady and they are less reactive, more responsive, although they can have a tendency to be resistant to change and need encouragement.

CARDINAL

ARIES, CANCER, LIBRA AND CAPRICORN ARE CARDINAL SIGNS

Their energy is often instinctive and action-oriented, enabling them to get things started, although there's sometimes a tendency to fail to carry things through.

MUTABLE

GEMINI, VIRGO, SAGITTARIUS AND PISCES ARE MUTABLE SIGNS

The clue here is their adaptability and responsiveness to change, which they don't fear, and readiness to listen to and embrace new ideas.

MERCURY RETROGRADE

This occurs several times over the astrological year and lasts for around four weeks, with a shadow week either side (a quick Google search will tell you the forthcoming dates). It's important what sign Mercury is in while it's retrograde, because its impact will be affected by the characteristics of that sign. For example, if Mercury is retrograde in Gemini, the sign of communication that is ruled by Mercury, the effect will be keenly felt in all areas of communication. However, if Mercury is retrograde in Aquarius, which rules the house of friendships and relationships, this may keenly affect our communication with large groups, or if in Sagittarius, which rules the house of travel, it could affect travel itineraries and encourage us to check our documents carefully.

Mercury retrograde can also be seen as an opportunity to pause, review or reconsider ideas and plans, to regroup, recalibrate and recuperate, and generally to take stock of where we are and how we might proceed. In our fast-paced 24/7 lives, Mercury retrograde can often be a useful opportunity to slow down and allow ourselves space to restore some necessary equilibrium.

SATURN RETURN

When the planet Saturn returns to the place in your chart that it occupied at the time of your birth, it has an impact. This occurs roughly every 28 years, so we can see immediately that it correlates with ages that we consider representative of different life stages and when we might anticipate change or adjustment to a different era. At 28 we can be considered at full adult maturity, probably established in our careers and relationships, maybe with children; at 56 we have reached middle age and are possibly at another of life's crossroads; and at 84, we might be considered at the full height of our wisdom, our lives almost complete. If you know the time and place of your birth date, an online Saturn return calculator can give you the exact timing.

It will also be useful to identify in which astrological sign Saturn falls in your chart, which will help you reflect on its influence, as both influences can be very illuminating about how you will experience and manage the impact of its return. Often the time leading up to a personal Saturn return is a demanding one, but the lessons learnt help inform the decisions made about how to progress your own goals. Don't fear this period, but work with its influence: knowledge is power and Saturn has a powerful energy you can harness should you choose.

THE MINOR PLANETS

Sun sign astrology seldom makes mention of these 'minor' planets that also orbit the sun, but increasingly their subtle influence is being referenced. If you have had your birth chart done (if you know your birth time and place you can do this online) you will have access to this additional information.

Like the 10 main planets on the previous pages, these 18 minor entities will also be positioned in an astrological sign, bringing their energy to bear on these characteristics. You may, for example, have Fortuna in Leo, or Diana in Sagittarius. Look to these for their subtle influences on your birth chart and life via the sign they inhabit, all of which will serve to animate and resonate further the information you can reference on your own personal journey.

AESCULAPIA

Jupiter's grandson and a powerful
healer, Aesculapia was taught by
Chiron and influences us in what
could be life-saving action, realised
through the characteristics of the sign
in which it falls in our chart.

BACCHUS

Jupiter's son, Bacchus is similarly
benevolent but can sometimes lack
restraint in the pursuit of pleasure.
How this plays out in your chart is
dependent on the sign in which
it falls.

APOLLO

Jupiter's son, gifted in art, music and
healing, Apollo rides the Sun across
the skies. His energy literally lights up
the way in which you inspire others,
characterised by the sign in which it
falls in your chart.

CERES

Goddess of agriculture and mother of
Proserpina, Ceres is associated with
the seasons and how we manage cycles
of change in our lives. This energy is
influenced by the sign in which it falls
in our chart.

CHIRON

Teacher of the gods, Chiron knew all about healing herbs and medical practices and he lends his energy to how we tackle the impossible or the unthinkable, that which seems difficult to do.

DIANA

Jupiter's independent daughter was allowed to run free without the shackles of marriage. Where this falls in your birth chart will indicate what you are not prepared to sacrifice in order to conform.

CUPID

Son of Venus. The sign into which Cupid falls will influence how you inspire love and desire in others, not always appropriately and sometimes illogically but it can still be an enduring passion.

FORTUNA

Jupiter's daughter, who is always shown blindfolded, influences your fated role in other people's lives, how you show up for them without really understanding why, and at the right time.

HYGEIA

Daughter of Aesculapia and also associated with health, Hygeia is about how you anticipate risk and the avoidance of unwanted outcomes. The way you do this is characterised by the sign in which Hygeia falls.

MINERVA

Another of Jupiter's daughters, depicted by an owl, will show you via the energy given to a particular astrological sign in your chart how you show up at your most intelligent and smart. How you operate intellectually.

JUNO

Juno was the wife of Jupiter and her position in your chart will indicate where you will make a commitment in order to feel safe and secure. It's where you might seek protection in order to flourish.

OPS

The wife of Saturn, Ops saved the life of her son Jupiter by giving her husband a stone to eat instead of him. Her energy in our chart enables us to find positive solutions to life's demands and dilemmas.

PANACEA

Gifted with healing powers, Panacea provides us with a remedy for all ills and difficulties, and how this plays out in your life will depend on the characteristics of the astrological sign in which her energy falls.

PSYCHE

Psyche, Venus' daughter-in-law, shows us that part of ourselves that is easy to love and endures through adversity, and your soul that survives death and flies free, like the butterfly that depicts her.

PROSERPINA

Daughter of Ceres, abducted by Pluto, Proserpina has to spend her life divided between earth and the underworld and she represents how we bridge the gulf between different and difficult aspects of our lives.

SALACIA

Neptune's wife, Salacia stands on the seashore bridging land and sea, happily bridging the two realities. In your chart, she shows how you can harmoniously bring two sides of yourself together.

VESTA

Daughter of Saturn, Vesta's job was to protect Rome and in turn she was protected by vestal virgins. Her energy influences how we manage our relationships with competitive females and male authority figures.

VULCAN

Vulcan was a blacksmith who knew how to control fire and fashion metal into shape, and through the sign in which it falls in your chart will show you how you control your passion and make it work for you.

FURTHER READING

Jung's Studies in Astrology: Prophecies, Magic and the Qualities of Time,

Liz Greene, Routledge (2018)

Lunar Oracle: Harness the Power of the Moon,

Liberty Phi, OH Editions (2021)

Metaphysics of Astrology: Why Astrology Works,

Ivan Antic, Independently published (2020)

*Parkers' Astrology: The Definitive Guide to Using Astrology in Every Aspect
of Your Life,*

Julia and Derek Parker, Dorling Kindersley (2020)

USEFUL WEBSITES

Alicebellastrology.com
Astro.com
Astrology.com
Cafeastrology.com
Costarastrology.com
Jessicaadams.com

USEFUL APPS

Astro Future
Co-Star
Moon
Sanctuary
Time Nomad
Time Passages

ACKNOWLEDGEMENTS

Thanks are due to my Taurean publisher Kate Pollard for commissioning this Astrology Oracle series, to Piscean Matt Tomlinson for his careful editing, and to Evi O Studio for their beautiful design and illustrations.

ABOUT THE AUTHOR

As a sun sign Aquarius Liberty Phi loves to explore the world and has lived on three different continents, currently residing in North America. Their Gemini moon inspires them to communicate their love of astrology and other esoteric practices while Leo rising helps energise them. Their first publication, also released by OH Editions, is a box set of 36 oracle cards and accompanying guide, entitled *Lunar Oracle: Harness the Power of the Moon*.

Published in 2023 by OH Editions,
an imprint of Welbeck Non-Fiction Ltd,
part of the Welbeck Publishing Group.
Offices in London, 20 Mortimer Street, London, W1T 3JW,
and Sydney, 205 Commonwealth Street, Surry Hills, 2010.
www.welbeckpublishing.com

Design © 2023 OH Editions
Text © 2023 Liberty Phi
Illustrations © 2023 Evi O. Studio

A CIP catalogue record for this book is available from the British Library.

ISBN 978-1-91431-796-5

Publisher: Kate Pollard
Editor: Sophie Elletson
In-house editor: Matt Tomlinson
Designer: Evi O. Studio
Illustrator: Evi O. Studio
Production controller: Jess Brisley
Printed and bound by Leo Paper

MIX
Paper | Supporting
responsible forestry
FSC® C020056
www.fsc.org

10 9 8 7 6 5 4 3 2 1